Emma's Busy D

Terry Cash

Coordinator of the Essex primary science
and technology advisory team

Illustrated by

Ian Newsham

Longman

Emma and her friends are having a busy day!

see page B

Badger has a fine set of new clothes!
Emma and Mouse paint a picture of him.

Which picture do you like best?
Would you use the same colours as Mouse?

What colour is Badger's hat in
Emma's picture?
What colour do you think Emma
will use for the tree?

Draw and colour a picture of your
house and garden.

Mouse asks Emma to make a dress for her.
She can't decide which colour to have.
Emma cuts out dress shapes for Mouse.
Rabbit wants a dress too.

4

see page B

Emma sticks the coloured dress shapes
on a piece of paper.
Mouse likes the red one best so Emma
draws a smiling face over it.
Which colour does Rabbit like best?

Cut out and colour some paper clothes.
Stick them on a large piece of paper.
Ask your family to choose a favourite colour.
Draw a face over the one each person chooses.
Which colour do most people like?

Emma has made a building from playbricks for Rabbit.

Can you make a building from playbricks for one of your toys?

see page B

Make some shapes like these.
Trace the shapes on this page.
Cut them out and colour them.

Rabbit has made a picture
with coloured shapes.

Stick your paper shapes on to
a piece of paper to make
a picture.

Rabbit asks Emma to build a wall for her.
She wants one that is strong
and will not fall down easily.

see
page
C

Emma has built one wall.
Rabbit has built another.

How are they different?

Rabbit wants to know which
is the strongest.

see page
C

Emma and Rabbit are seeing which wall is best.

Emma is trying to blow her wall down. Rabbit is rolling marbles against his wall.

Build 2 walls like Emma's and Rabbit's. Try to blow each wall down.

Roll marbles against each wall. Which is the strongest?

Badger has made a Robot.
They are playing in the rain.
The rain is making Robot go wrong.

Emma is trying to find some clothes
to keep Robot dry.

Which ones should she choose?

see
page
D

13

Poor little Robot won't work properly if he gets wet. How can he get across the lake to go to the party?

Badger and Emma have an idea.

see page E

the boat

You can make a boat for Robot.
Find some things that float well.

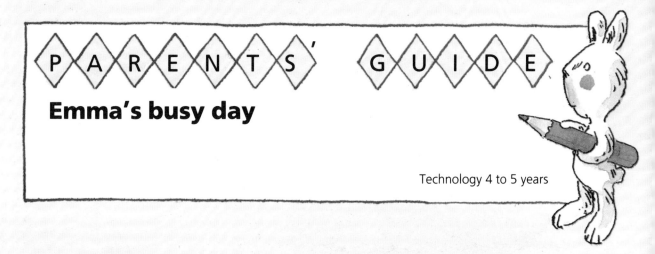

Dear Parent,

Emma's Busy Day introduces children to the many skills and concepts that are developed within the National Curriculum programmes of study and attainment targets for Technology with Design.

This is a new curriculum area for all schools and should not be confused with craft work; neither should it be considered as a part of the science commitment that all schools are required to meet. Science and mathematics have much to contribute to technology, but technology exists in its own right and is concerned with identifying needs and opportunities, generating and developing design proposals, planning and making (which itself is not just limited to making things, artefacts, but designing and implementing proposals for developing systems and environments too) and evaluating the outcomes of the work.

Much of the work in technology, particularly for younger children, will be aimed at encouraging independence and self-reliance. It is most important that any activities undertaken in this book should be attempted without undue pressure. Your child should be encouraged to try things, but the experience should be an enjoyable one. The child is not seeking right answers with any of the activities, but should be exploring a wide range of possibilities.

By entering into the spirit of investigation your child will be developing important skills, such as careful, logical thought, the correct use of simple tools, an increased awareness of the various properties of a wide range of household materials and adhesives, as well as an appreciation of the important part played by technology in our rapidly changing world.

A

Pages 2—3

Attainment target 2 Generating a design

An important aspect of technology is design, and developing an awareness and appreciation of colour and shape is crucial. Use the activities on pages 2 and 3 as an opportunity to talk with your child about his or her own ideas and suggestions. Choices of colour are left to your child so discuss these choices, but be prepared to accept whatever is suggested; there are no right or wrong answers, just preferences.

Pages 4—5

Attainment target 1 Identifying needs and opportunities

Let everyone in the family enter into the spirit of this investigation, which is to take part in a simple survey concerned with colour preference for clothes. The more people your child can ask, the more interesting will be the result. 'Market research' and an awareness of other people's likes and dislikes is important in the design stages of any technological project.

Pages 6—8

Attainment target 3 Planning and making

It is possible to buy packets of gummed simple geometric shapes in bold, primary colours. However, if you cannot obtain any, the shapes can be cut from plain paper. Let your child take a leading role in cutting out and colouring the shapes. Using two-dimensional shapes to represent a three dimensional world is an important visual concept. If your child has play bricks made from similar shapes, an excellent extension to the activity would be to make a simple 3-D model from the bricks, then to record the shape using the cut-out shapes glued to a sheet of paper.

Page 9

A significant component of National Curriculum technology is the ability to build and test. This investigation asks your child to build a wall from play bricks. Once again it must be stressed that it is important that your child should attempt this unaided. No matter how much you feel you would like to direct the activity, particularly if your child is experiencing some difficulty, offer encouragement only. Children must feel from the outset that they are not seeking 'right' answers to please you, but that they have a right to choose, to have an opinion of their own and that when things go wrong this is not seen as failure, merely part of the learning process. Children must be given the confidence to feel that they are independent learners.

Pages 10–11

Building the tallest possible tower is an activity that will be enjoyed and which introduces problems of stability and careful design and construction. This activity will also encourage greater dexterity and manipulative skills.

  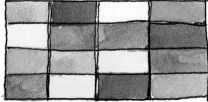

As an extension of the exercise in wall building, ask your child to copy these brick patterns. Some children will be able to follow the patterns quite easily, but do not be concerned if your child finds difficulty. Such spatial awareness and appreciation of pattern takes time to develop. Testing by blowing or rolling a ball is a very arbitrary test, perhaps you could discuss other possibilities. Ask your child if it was a 'fair' test, or might there be a fairer way. Follow up any suggestions, but if none are forthcoming don't pursue the matter at this time.

C

Page 12

Encourage your child to make his or her own robot. The robot puppet shown here introduces a number of important concepts, such as moving joints and articulation. If your child enjoys making this little puppet, encourage him or her to design and make a different robot, perhaps modelled on a favourite fictional character, or even themselves. Similar moving puppets can also be used to create a shadow puppet play by moving them behind a sheet with a strong light shining directly at it in a dimly lit room. This activity will encourage creative play and language development as characters are made to act out scenarios and are given voices to develop the plot.

D

Page 13

Here your child is encouraged to make choices from examples of articles of clothing, identifying those that would keep someone dry. This activity can be done in a far better way by gathering together some of your child's own clothes and asking him or her to sort the pile into those that keep you warm, those that keep you dry and perhaps others that would be cool to wear when it is hot. Get your child to talk about the various choices, why he or she thinks a particular fabric would be best suited for one purpose rather than another. In this way an awareness of variety in materials and their different properties is being developed.

Pages 14–17

This investigation is NOT designed to produce a perfect model boat, but rather to explore a variety of different materials to discover things that sink and others that will float. Let your child spend some time simply playing with a wide variety of things to see what each might do. Some things will float while they have air inside (bottles, saucers, lids) but if they are filled with water they may sink. Similarly, some things that sink may actually float if placed into the water in a different way. When your child is ready to make a simple boat, let him or her choose just a few things that float well. These may be joined together with tape, string or glue, or may simply be balanced one on another. A perfectly adequate 'boat' that will carry a small toy could be nothing more than a polystyrene tray or a lump of wood, but if it works to your child's satisfaction that is perfectly adequate at this stage.

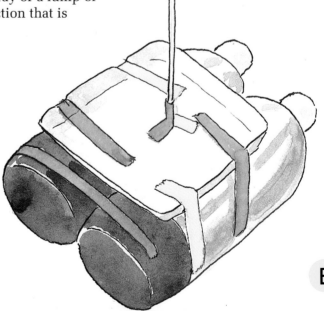

E

Pages 18–23

Relating an animal's size and shape to that of a chair is simply raising an awareness of differences for children. Look around the home and discuss the different sizes of furniture that there may be, from a baby's high chair and cot to a large, comfortable settee. Your child could also make some play furniture for a favourite soft toy, matching the sizes as necessary, or a play house as here:

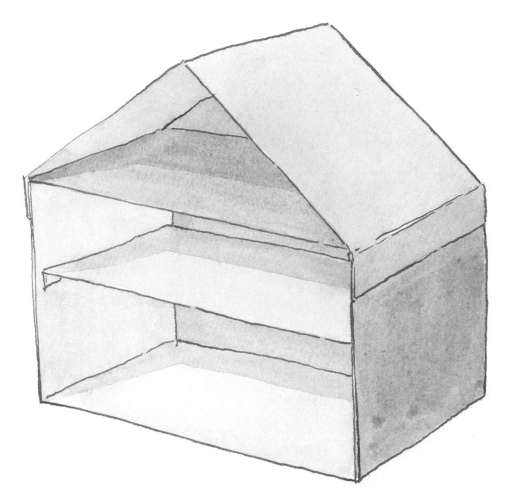

A perfectly adequate play house can be made from a large cardboard box with little or no modification. It is the way in which the 'house' is used to develop creative play that is more important. The 'furniture' can be very simple, using an empty box as a bed and yogurt pots as chairs.

Pages 24–25

Let your child watch an egg being boiled to appreciate how long 3 to 4 minutes actually lasts. It will seem like a very long time. Making simple timers is an interesting activity. They need not be used to time specific things such as eggs, but could be used to time simple activities such as the number of beads that your child can thread on a lace, the number of marbles that can be flipped into a tin or any other simple, repetitive task to encourage speed and dexterity.

A water clock can be made, using an empty margarine tub that sinks slowly in a bowl of water, with something to weigh it down (stones, plasticine, marbles etc.) so that the water level is just above the level of the hole made in the tub.

With all timers, whether using water, sand or salt, the period of time can be altered by experimenting with different sized holes. Suggest that your child makes a timer that times a brief period and compare that with one designed to time a longer period.

G

Pages 26–27

An extension of the skittles game would be 'roll a ball' made from 5 boxes with holes cut into each one and numbered for scoring.

The games are very simple to make, but are enjoyable to play, which reinforces another important concept within National Curriculum technology. Designing and making things is only part of the process; testing and modifying to achieve a better product is just as important, as is the idea of evaluating the end product. In this case the evaluation process comes with the enjoyment of playing the game.

Pages 28–32

Sequencing of events is an important organisational skill. This exercise is designed to develop logical thought. The child is required to think through the process of getting ready for bed and the various stages that this implies. For example, one would not wash or bath before undressing nor eat and drink after cleaning teeth. Discuss the various stages, but let your child work through the sequence without too much prompting.

Tape a plastic or polystyrene tray
to 2 empty lemonade bottles.

Does your boat float in the bath?
Will it carry a small toy safely?

Mouse has invited Badger to tea.
What is happening?
Why is mouse upset?

see page F

Emma is sorry for Mouse
and Badger. She has made
a chair for Badger and
then she shows Mouse how to
make some more furniture.

Small boxes make good beds. Fill them with cotton wool or material. A piece of card can be stuck on for a headboard.

Matchboxes make good drawers. Stick them together like this to make a chest of drawers.

Now everyone wants to come to tea.
They have brought their chairs with them
but they have got muddled up.

Can you sort them out?

Which animal should sit on which chair?

Rabbit is boiling eggs for tea.
Piglet is making bread soldiers.
Rabbit has made a sand timer to help
him boil the eggs.

see page G

Make your own sand timer.

You will need
2 yogurt pots
and some salt.

Make a hole in the
bottom of one pot.

Fill the pot with the
hole in it with salt.

Hold it over the other
pot and watch the salt
pour through.

Try using sand or water instead of salt.
What happens if you make the hole larger?

After tea Emma and her friends
play skittles.
Emma finds 6 empty lemonade
bottles and 3 balls.
She paints big numbers on
each bottle.

They each roll 3 balls and try
to knock down the skittles.

You can make your own skittles
and play a game.

Set up your skittles like Emma
and her friends have.

see page H

Everyone is tired now.
They start getting ready for bed.

Who will be in bed first?
Who will be in bed last?

28

see page H

Emma is getting ready for bed but
something is wrong.
These pictures are in the wrong order.

Put the pictures in the right order.

Emma and her friends are all tucked up in bed.
They are very tired.
They have had a very busy day!